MW00881585

The Bible Reading and Prayer Journal

40 Days of Following Jesus

TOM HOGSED

Scripture Usage
Scripture quotations marked ESV are from the ESV® Bible (The Holy Bible, English Standard Version®), copyright © 2001 by Crossway, a publishing ministry of Good News Publishers. Used by permission. All rights reserved.

All Scripture quotations marked NKJV are taken from the New King James Version®, copyright © 1982 by Thomas Nelson. Used by permission. All rights reserved.

Scripture quotations marked NLT are taken from the Holy Bible, New Living Translation, copyright ©1996, 2004, 2015 by Tyndale House Foundation. Used by permission of Tyndale House Publishers, Inc., Carol Stream, Illinois 60188. All rights reserved.

Book Cover
Design: Inspired by Black and Green Modern Minimalist Art Exhibit Event Program by Marketplace Designers via canva.com

DEDICATION

If you are a follower of Jesus, you should have a desire to spend time getting to know Him. God has given us His written word so that we can know and be known by Him. Paul wrote to the young pastor Timothy concerning the purpose and outcome of reading and applying Scripture.

> "All Scripture is inspired by God and is useful to
> teach us what is true and to make us realize what is
> wrong in our lives. It corrects us when we are
> wrong and teaches us to do what is right. God uses
> it to prepare and equip his people to do every
> good work." (2 Timothy 3:16-17, NLT)

Interacting with God's Word allows you to discover the keys to living the way God intended. Sometimes your calendar and priorities get in the way of quality and quantity time with God, but you must fight for designated time with Him every day. We typically have no problem scrolling through social media feeds, binge-watching favorite shows, or reserving time for hobbies and things we enjoy. Spiritual disciplines must become a habit. They must be a priority.

Spiritual disciplines don't become habits overnight. You must stay consistent and quickly pick yourself up if you get off track. I am challenging you to stick with this journal for the entire 40 days.

It will be hard. It will take determination. It will take commitment.

But, you CAN do it.

If you choose to finish the entire 40 days, consider this book dedicated to YOU. I'm simply providing a resource. God is providing the truth. You are spending time with God each day, which has the potential to change the direction of your life.

TABLE OF CONTENTS

ACKNOWLEDGMENTS

Through the years God has allowed me to work with hundreds of people and I can honestly say that I LOVE to write books and create resources. Why? Because I am motivated by seeing people connect with God in a personal way. I believe getting people to experience God through spiritual disciplines is part of my calling in life.

I want to thank my current church family, The Summit Church, for always extending grace to me as I explore God's giftings in my life. I pray that God uses me in your life as He has used you in mine.

I truly love each one of you and pray that this journal will provide a starting or continuing point for your faith. The spiritual disciplines in this book have the potential to move you from where you are to where God wants you to be.

Thank you for being a group of people who make it enjoyable to be a pastor!

HOW TO SPEND TIME WITH GOD

Chances are that no one has ever allowed you to spend a few days or weeks observing their time with God…to see how they read the Bible, journal, memorize Scripture, and pray.

It makes sense because spending time with God is typically a private habit, not one to be flaunted in front of others. However, I have discovered that there are people who want to spend time with God, but may not know where to start or how to do it.

I want to give you a quick inside look at how I spend time with God, although you may not choose to approach spiritual disciplines just like me.

The key to spiritual disciplines is not how you do it, but if you do it. Action trumps intention every time.

I would love to tell you that I am approaching this topic as someone who always gets it right and is as consistent as he should be in spending time with God, but I'm not. Sometimes I struggle with staying focused on daily spiritual disciplines. There have even been seasons throughout my life when I have found myself willingly neglecting time with God. I'm not proud of those seasons since ignoring God's voice and my relationship with Him means that something or someone else was receiving my attention.

No matter if you are new to faith or it's been a part of your life for a long time, it is helpful to be reminded of *what spiritual disciplines are* and *why they are important.*

Dr. Don Whitney, author of *Spiritual Disciplines for the Christian Life* and *Praying the Bible*, answers the question, "What are the spiritual disciplines?"

> The spiritual disciplines are those practices found in Scripture that promote spiritual growth among believers in the gospel of Jesus Christ. They are habits of devotion, habits of experiential Christianity that have been practiced by God's people since biblical times.[1]

In my opinion the most influential and transformational spiritual disciplines are:

1) **Reading the Bible** (God Speaking To You)
2) **Praying** (You Speaking To God)
3) **Memorizing Scripture** (God Shaping the Way You Think)
4) **Obeying God** (You Changing the Way You Act).

These are not the *only* disciplines but we can clearly see them modeled in the life of Jesus, who is the ultimate example of Someone who lived in full obedience to God the Father.

Why are spiritual disciplines important?

If we remove the word *spiritual*, we are left with the word *disciplines*, or just discipline. Merriam-Webster defines the word *discipline* as training that corrects, molds, or perfects the mental faculties or moral character.[2]

---

[1] Whitney, Don. "What Are Spiritual Disciplines?" *Ask Pastor John*. December 31, 2015. https://www.desiringgod.org/interviews/what-are-spiritual-disciplines
[2] Merriam-Webster (online dictionary). Definition for the word *discipline*. https://www.merriam-webster.com/dictionary/discipline

Practicing spiritual disciplines correct, mold, and perfect the way we live in relationship with God and others. These habits give God the opportunity to change us from *who we are* into *who He wants us to be*.

There wasn't really anyone in my life who let me "sit in" on the time they spent with God. There were people who *told me how to spend time with God*, but I did not learn through *observation*. It is similar to someone having *book knowledge*, but not *experiential knowledge*. I was left to formulate my own practices of spiritual disciplines. Although there's nothing wrong with discovering spiritual disciplines through trial and error, I believe many people are looking for tangible examples of how to spend time with God.

Using the spiritual disciplines above, I'm going to give you an inside look at how I spend time with God. It's not the *only* way, but it is *a* way.

Spiritual Discipline #1
Reading the Bible (God Speaking To You)

There are 3 keys to making Bible Reading a priority.

1. ***Have a place.*** If reading the Bible is left to "if you have time or when you have time" it will never become a habit. You may have to wake up earlier, change around what you do at lunch, do it as soon as you get home from work, or give yourself time before you go to bed.

   No matter what, you must have a time and place that is relatively unchanging. I typically schedule time immediately after breakfast. You must have a plan to read your Bible. Benjamin Franklin is attributed with saying, "Failing to plan is planning to fail." Reading the Bible daily will take hard work, but you can do hard things.

2. *Have a plan*. I do not think that reading random Bible verses is a good plan. If you are doing that right now, let me challenge you to find a plan. The best plans are ones that take you through a book of the Bible, part of the Bible, or the whole Bible. God didn't intend for His Word to be approached the same way we approach social media news feeds – randomly moving from one thing to the next. YouVersion (a free online Bible app and website) has some incredible plans. I have also published several books that take you through books of the Bible. You can view the books I have available on Amazon by visiting my author page at amazon.com/author/tomhogsed.

It may also be helpful to consider two other things when reading the Bible. **Choose a good translation**. I prefer the ESV (English Standard Version) for most of the Bible, but I also enjoy the way the Old Testament and the Gospels read in the NLT (New Living Translation). **Invest in a study Bible or commentary**. In the back of this book, I provide a *Bible Reading Resource List* which will help you acquire some extra help when you encounter some verses that you don't understand.

Let me also mention that the number of chapters you read per day is not the celebration point. Knowledge, application, and a relationship with God is the celebration point.

3. *Have a pen*. Writing or journaling your responses to reading the Bible takes you beyond *reading* and moves you to *thinking, applying, and obeying*. I have spent many years journaling through the entire New Testament and several books in the Old Testament. I would love to tell you that I have properly obeyed and applied all that I have read, but I

still fall very short in many areas of my life. However, writing out my thoughts and responses has helped me tremendously. How much do you have to write?

Start with a couple sentences a day and allow the amount of journaling to grow. This habit also allows you to look back and see how God has been working in your life.

Spiritual Discipline #2
Praying (You Speaking To God)

Prayer is one that I continue to neglect more than I'd like to admit, but it is our lifeline of communication with God.

The Bible is how God speaks to us and prayer is how we speak to God.

Prayer is vital in developing this relationship with God, not just a one-sided conversation. If you are just starting out (or have even been practicing prayer for a while), I'd like to challenge you to merge Bible reading and prayer. Many times we separate them, but since relational development and obedience is the goal, I believe God wants them to go hand in hand.

Take, for instance, Psalm 139.

> Search me, O God, and know my heart! Try me and know my thoughts! And see if there be any grievous way in me, and lead me in the way everlasting! (Psalm 139:23-24, ESV)

Instead of continuing to read on in the Bible, stop in the moment and ask God to search your heart for anything that shouldn't be there. This gives God the opportunity to bring to remembrance any sins in your life and you the chance to confess them. Every human conversation works like this – one speaks and one listens and then it is reversed. God created us in His image, so I believe that He desires the same conversational interaction He has given us with other human beings.

I'm not steering you away from keeping any type of prayer list because it is valuable for you to write down prayer requests. In fact, be sure to use the **Prayer Request Journal** in the back of this book. You can simply write down things you are praying about and then record when God has answered your prayer.

I would also like to give you something else that will help those of you who may not know how to pray the Bible. I have created a **Guide To Prayer** that will lead you in praying right from the Bible. It is a very helpful resource for praying.

I also find myself using a book called *The Valley of Vision: A Collection of Puritan Prayers and Devotions*. "This book has been prepared not to 'supply' prayers but to prompt and encourage the Christian as he treads the path on which others have gone before." I do find myself praying some of these written prayers as they seem to be birthed out of the soul.[3]

---

[3] Bennett, Arthur (editor), The Valley of Vision: A Collection of Puritan Prayers and Devotions (Carlisle, PA: The Banner of Truth Trust, 1975).

Discipline #3
Memorizing Scripture (God Shaping the Way You Think)

I have a lot of stuff memorized – song lyrics (I like 80's music!), favorite lines in TV and movies, and all kinds of other random phrases. What I have discovered is that *frequent exposure to words we care about will result in memorization.* How many random song lyrics or movie lines do you know? Probably quite a few…and most without even trying.

Thanks to churches, Sunday school programs, school, and college, I have had lots of experience memorizing Scripture. There are many benefits to committing Scripture to memory – helps during temptation, gives peace during hardship, grows our love for God's words, and fills our minds with the truth. If we were to combine all of the benefits, they could be summarized into one advantage – *memorizing Scripture gives God a consistent voice at any and every moment of the day.* You may not always have instant access to a Bible, but your mind is instantly accessible. God can bring to mind those words you have committed to memory and use them at the right moment.

One of my secrets to memorizing Scripture has been an app called Bible Memory. Although some of you may prefer an "old-school" approach to Scripture memorization, this app (biblememory.com) has kept me on track with not only memorizing verses, but also reviewing them. I will say that this has been a BIG challenge for me so you may want to begin with an attainable goal, such as memorizing one verse a week or month. For those of you who have gotten apathetic in your faith, please consider challenging your faith this year through filling your mind with God's Word.

Discipline #4

Obeying God (You Changing the Way You Act)

This is where we conclude. Reading God's Word, praying, and memorizing Scripture should push you toward mind and life change. Hearing from God, responding to Him, and filling your mind with truth has the potential to show you what it means to live as Jesus lived...in full obedience to God the Father. Life change is not an giant leap from *Point A* to *Point B* but a series of small, daily steps in the right direction.

Spiritual disciplines are not the pursuit, but the means by which we come to know and be known by God.

HOW TO USE THIS JOURNAL

The GOAL for this journal is to **help you better organize the time you spend with God**. The journal brings 4 Spiritual Disciplines into one place so that you can focus on spending time with God rather than trying to discover how to do it.

To refresh your memory, here are the **4 Spiritual Disciplines** you will be practicing for the next 40 days – 1) Bible Reading, 2) Praying, 3) Memorizing Scripture, and 4) Obeying God.

You may be tempted to skip one of these disciplines, but I want to challenge you to put in the hard work and practice all four of these disciplines for the next 40 days.

Here is what you need to do BEFORE you begin your 40-day journey to following Jesus:

Choose a Bible Reading Plan
This is the most important part since these are the readings that will direct your thinking over the next several weeks. In the back of this book you will find a few suggestions for **Bible Reading Plans** or you can choose one from bible.com/reading-plans. It's also possible that you may have a devotional book or another resource to help guide you. You can even pick a book or two out of the Bible and read a chapter each day. Although it is important to choose a solid plan, the most essential piece is that you are reading God's Word each day. If you would like a reading plan that also helps you think a little deeper about the Scriptures, consider picking up one of my books at amazon.com/author/tomhogsed.

In case you need some additional resources to help you understand the Bible, I have included a chapter at the end of this book called **Bible Reading Resource List**.

Pick Verses to Memorize

I have provided some **suggested verses to memorize** in the back of this book. You can also choose any verse you would like, but make sure you are committed to memorizing at least one verse a week. As I mentioned earlier, I use an app called Bible Memory. It helps keep me on track with the verses I am memorizing.

Prepare to Pray

In addition to the daily prayer journaling, I have provided two resources in the back of this book: **Guide to Prayer** and a **Prayer Request Journal**. These will help those of you who may not know what to pray about or how to organize all of your prayer requests. The **Guide to Prayer** gives you very specific prayers to pray from Scripture. The **Prayer Request Journal** gives you a place to write down personal requests – it's like a list of your prayers.

Take Notes on Sermons

I believe that another vital part of developing your spiritual disciplines is being connected to a local church. Every week I provide you with a journal entry for sermon notes, which means that you should take this book with you to church and take notes on the pastor's message. Why? Listening to someone teach from the Bible has a way of helping you examine your spiritual health. So once a week, take notes on the sermon and then write down one way you can apply what you have heard.

Treat Yourself to a Nice Pen

This may sound odd, but I have a designated pen for my Bible journaling. You are going to be doing a fair amount of writing each day and it's important to have a pen attached to the cover of this book. This prevents you from having to search for a pen every time you need to journal. Personally, I prefer the Micron pens because of how they write and I think it makes my writing look neater!

Follow My Example

This may seem like a lot of information, but I know you will be able to do this! In case you are still unsure of how this works, I'm going to give you a "Sample Journal Entry" so you can see how I do this.

SAMPLE JOURNAL ENTRY
THE BIBLE READING AND PRAYER JOURNAL

BIBLE READING
God Speaking To You

What Scripture did you read today? *2 Corinthians 1:3-11*

What was your favorite verse in today's reading? *2 Corinthians 1:4*

JOURNALING
Writing Your Thoughts

What is Scripture saying to you about who God is (His character), what He has done (His works), or what He will do (His promises)?

God is said to be a God of mercies and comfort. I looked up the word mercies and it means "compassion or forgiveness shown toward someone whom it is within one's power to punish or harm." This means that He has shown me forgiveness, even when I didn't deserve it. God also comforts me, which means He brings peace when my circumstances are not peaceful.

Briefly describe what you learned in your Bible reading today.

Because God is a God of mercy, I should also be looking for ways to show mercy to others even when they have done wrong against me. Verse 4 says that God comforts us in our affliction so we will know how to comfort others. These two characteristics of God should be demonstrated in my life every day.

OBEYING
Changing the Way You Act

How will your thoughts, actions, or reactions change based on today's Scripture reading?
I have recently been holding on to issues of anger I have with a few people in my life. I need to reconcile with these individuals so I can show mercy as God has showed me mercy. I also know someone in my family who has just experienced a loss and I am going to reach out to them today to see if I can encourage them.

MEMORIZING
God Shaping the Way You Think

Your goal is to memorize one verse every 7 days. What Scripture verse are you memorizing this week? *Romans 8:28*

PRAYING
You Speaking To God

Thank You for *showing me mercy and comforting me during my times of hardship*

Forgive me for *failing to show mercy to those who have wronged me. You have freely forgiven me so help me to forgive others.*

Help me to *see people who are in need and bring comfort into their life by listening and taking action.*

Additional prayers or thoughts: _____

_____

_____

Don't forget to use the **Prayer Request Journal** and **Guide to Prayer** in the back of this book.

DAY 1
THE BIBLE READING AND PRAYER JOURNAL

BIBLE READING
God Speaking To You

What Scripture did you read today? _____

What was your favorite verse in today's reading? _____

JOURNALING
Writing Your Thoughts

What is Scripture saying to you about who God is (His character),
what He has done (His works), or what He will do (His promises)?

_____

_____

_____

_____

_____

Briefly describe what you learned in your Bible reading today.

_____

_____

_____

_____

_____

_____

OBEYING
Changing the Way You Act

How will your thoughts, actions, or reactions change based on today's Scripture reading?

_____

_____

_____

_____

_____

MEMORIZING
God Shaping the Way You Think

Your goal is to memorize one verse every 7 days. What Scripture verse are you memorizing this week? _____

PRAYING
You Speaking To God

Thank You for _____

_____

Forgive me for _____

_____

Help me to _____

_____

Additional prayers or thoughts: _____

_____

_____

Don't forget to use the **Prayer Request Journal** and **Guide to Prayer** in the back of this book.

DAY 2
THE BIBLE READING AND PRAYER JOURNAL

BIBLE READING
God Speaking To You

What Scripture did you read today? _____

What was your favorite verse in today's reading? _____

JOURNALING
Writing Your Thoughts

What is Scripture saying to you about who God is (His character), what He has done (His works), or what He will do (His promises)?

_____

_____

_____

_____

_____

Briefly describe what you learned in your Bible reading today.

_____

_____

_____

_____

_____

_____

OBEYING
Changing the Way You Act

How will your thoughts, actions, or reactions change based on today's Scripture reading?

_____

_____

_____

_____

_____

MEMORIZING
God Shaping the Way You Think

Your goal is to memorize one verse every 7 days. What Scripture verse are you memorizing this week? _____

PRAYING
You Speaking To God

Thank You for _____

_____

Forgive me for _____

_____

Help me to _____

_____

Additional prayers or thoughts: _____

_____

_____

Don't forget to use the **Prayer Request Journal** and **Guide to Prayer** in the back of this book.

DAY 3
THE BIBLE READING AND PRAYER JOURNAL

BIBLE READING
God Speaking To You

What Scripture did you read today? _____

What was your favorite verse in today's reading? _____

JOURNALING
Writing Your Thoughts

What is Scripture saying to you about who God is (His character), what He has done (His works), or what He will do (His promises)?

_____

_____

_____

_____

Briefly describe what you learned in your Bible reading today.

_____

_____

_____

_____

_____

_____

OBEYING
Changing the Way You Act

How will your thoughts, actions, or reactions change based on today's Scripture reading?

_____

_____

_____

_____

_____

MEMORIZING
God Shaping the Way You Think

Your goal is to memorize one verse every 7 days. What Scripture verse are you memorizing this week? _____

PRAYING
You Speaking To God

Thank You for _____

_____

Forgive me for _____

_____

Help me to _____

_____

Additional prayers or thoughts: _____

_____

_____

Don't forget to use the **Prayer Request Journal** and **Guide to Prayer** in the back of this book.

DAY 4
THE BIBLE READING AND PRAYER JOURNAL

BIBLE READING
God Speaking To You

What Scripture did you read today? _____

What was your favorite verse in today's reading? _____

JOURNALING
Writing Your Thoughts

What is Scripture saying to you about who God is (His character), what He has done (His works), or what He will do (His promises)?

_____

_____

_____

_____

_____

Briefly describe what you learned in your Bible reading today.

_____

_____

_____

_____

_____

_____

OBEYING
Changing the Way You Act

How will your thoughts, actions, or reactions change based on today's Scripture reading?

_____

_____

_____

_____

_____

MEMORIZING
God Shaping the Way You Think

Your goal is to memorize one verse every 7 days. What Scripture verse are you memorizing this week? _____

PRAYING
You Speaking To God

Thank You for _____

_____

Forgive me for _____

_____

Help me to _____

_____

Additional prayers or thoughts: _____

_____

_____

Don't forget to use the **Prayer Request Journal** and **Guide to Prayer** in the back of this book.

DAY 5

THE BIBLE READING AND PRAYER JOURNAL

BIBLE READING
God Speaking To You

What Scripture did you read today? _____

What was your favorite verse in today's reading? _____

JOURNALING
Writing Your Thoughts

What is Scripture saying to you about who God is (His character), what He has done (His works), or what He will do (His promises)?

_____

_____

_____

_____

_____

Briefly describe what you learned in your Bible reading today.

_____

_____

_____

_____

_____

_____

OBEYING
Changing the Way You Act

How will your thoughts, actions, or reactions change based on today's Scripture reading?

_____

_____

_____

_____

_____

MEMORIZING
God Shaping the Way You Think

Your goal is to memorize one verse every 7 days. What Scripture verse are you memorizing this week? _____

PRAYING
You Speaking To God

Thank You for _____

_____

Forgive me for _____

_____

Help me to _____

_____

Additional prayers or thoughts: _____

_____

_____

Don't forget to use the **Prayer Request Journal** and **Guide to Prayer** in the back of this book.

DAY 6
THE BIBLE READING AND PRAYER JOURNAL

BIBLE READING
God Speaking To You

What Scripture did you read today? _____

What was your favorite verse in today's reading? _____

JOURNALING
Writing Your Thoughts

What is Scripture saying to you about who God is (His character),
what He has done (His works), or what He will do (His promises)?

_____

_____

_____

_____

Briefly describe what you learned in your Bible reading today.

_____

_____

_____

_____

_____

_____

OBEYING
Changing the Way You Act

How will your thoughts, actions, or reactions change based on today's Scripture reading?

_____

_____

_____

_____

_____

MEMORIZING
God Shaping the Way You Think

Your goal is to memorize one verse every 7 days. What Scripture verse are you memorizing this week? _____

PRAYING
You Speaking To God

Thank You for _____

_____

Forgive me for _____

_____

Help me to _____

_____

Additional prayers or thoughts: _____

_____

_____

Don't forget to use the **Prayer Request Journal** and **Guide to Prayer** in the back of this book.

DAY 7

THE BIBLE READING AND PRAYER JOURNAL

BIBLE READING
God Speaking To You

What Scripture did you read today? _____

What was your favorite verse in today's reading? _____

JOURNALING
Writing Your Thoughts

What is Scripture saying to you about who God is (His character), what He has done (His works), or what He will do (His promises)?

_____

_____

_____

_____

_____

Briefly describe what you learned in your Bible reading today.

_____

_____

_____

_____

_____

_____

OBEYING
Changing the Way You Act

How will your thoughts, actions, or reactions change based on today's Scripture reading?

_____

_____

_____

_____

_____

MEMORIZING
God Shaping the Way You Think

Your goal is to memorize one verse every 7 days. What Scripture verse are you memorizing this week? _____

PRAYING
You Speaking To God

Thank You for _____

_____

Forgive me for _____

_____

Help me to _____

_____

Additional prayers or thoughts: _____

_____

_____

Don't forget to use the **Prayer Request Journal** and **Guide to Prayer** in the back of this book.

DAY 8

THE BIBLE READING AND PRAYER JOURNAL

BIBLE READING
God Speaking To You

What Scripture did you read today? _____

What was your favorite verse in today's reading? _____

JOURNALING
Writing Your Thoughts

What is Scripture saying to you about who God is (His character), what He has done (His works), or what He will do (His promises)?

_____

_____

_____

_____

Briefly describe what you learned in your Bible reading today.

_____

_____

_____

_____

_____

_____

OBEYING
Changing the Way You Act

How will your thoughts, actions, or reactions change based on today's Scripture reading?

_____

_____

_____

_____

_____

MEMORIZING
God Shaping the Way You Think

Your goal is to memorize one verse every 7 days. What Scripture verse are you memorizing this week? _____

PRAYING
You Speaking To God

Thank You for _____

_____

Forgive me for _____

_____

Help me to _____

_____

Additional prayers or thoughts: _____

_____

_____

Don't forget to use the **Prayer Request Journal** and **Guide to Prayer** in the back of this book.

DAY 9

THE BIBLE READING AND PRAYER JOURNAL

BIBLE READING
God Speaking To You

What Scripture did you read today? _____

What was your favorite verse in today's reading? _____

JOURNALING
Writing Your Thoughts

What is Scripture saying to you about who God is (His character), what He has done (His works), or what He will do (His promises)?

_____

_____

_____

_____

_____

Briefly describe what you learned in your Bible reading today.

_____

_____

_____

_____

_____

_____

OBEYING
Changing the Way You Act

How will your thoughts, actions, or reactions change based on today's Scripture reading?

_____

_____

_____

_____

_____

MEMORIZING
God Shaping the Way You Think

Your goal is to memorize one verse every 7 days. What Scripture verse are you memorizing this week? _____

PRAYING
You Speaking To God

Thank You for _____

_____

Forgive me for _____

_____

Help me to _____

_____

Additional prayers or thoughts: _____

_____

_____

Don't forget to use the **Prayer Request Journal** and **Guide to Prayer** in the back of this book.

DAY 10

THE BIBLE READING AND PRAYER JOURNAL

BIBLE READING
God Speaking To You

What Scripture did you read today? _____

What was your favorite verse in today's reading? _____

JOURNALING
Writing Your Thoughts

What is Scripture saying to you about who God is (His character), what He has done (His works), or what He will do (His promises)?

_____

_____

_____

_____

_____

Briefly describe what you learned in your Bible reading today.

_____

_____

_____

_____

_____

_____

OBEYING
Changing the Way You Act

How will your thoughts, actions, or reactions change based on today's Scripture reading?

_____

_____

_____

_____

_____

MEMORIZING
God Shaping the Way You Think

Your goal is to memorize one verse every 7 days. What Scripture verse are you memorizing this week? _____

PRAYING
You Speaking To God

Thank You for _____

_____

Forgive me for _____

_____

Help me to _____

_____

Additional prayers or thoughts: _____

_____

_____

Don't forget to use the **Prayer Request Journal** and **Guide to Prayer** in the back of this book.

DAY 11
THE BIBLE READING AND PRAYER JOURNAL

BIBLE READING
God Speaking To You

What Scripture did you read today? _____

What was your favorite verse in today's reading? _____

JOURNALING
Writing Your Thoughts

What is Scripture saying to you about who God is (His character), what He has done (His works), or what He will do (His promises)?

_____

_____

_____

_____

_____

Briefly describe what you learned in your Bible reading today.

_____

_____

_____

_____

_____

_____

OBEYING
Changing the Way You Act

How will your thoughts, actions, or reactions change based on today's Scripture reading?

_____

_____

_____

_____

_____

MEMORIZING
God Shaping the Way You Think

Your goal is to memorize one verse every 7 days. What Scripture verse are you memorizing this week? _____

PRAYING
You Speaking To God

Thank You for _____

_____

Forgive me for _____

_____

Help me to _____

_____

Additional prayers or thoughts: _____

_____

_____

Don't forget to use the **Prayer Request Journal** and **Guide to Prayer** in the back of this book.

DAY 12

THE BIBLE READING AND PRAYER JOURNAL

BIBLE READING
God Speaking To You

What Scripture did you read today? _____

What was your favorite verse in today's reading? _____

JOURNALING
Writing Your Thoughts

What is Scripture saying to you about who God is (His character), what He has done (His works), or what He will do (His promises)?

_____

_____

_____

_____

_____

Briefly describe what you learned in your Bible reading today.

_____

_____

_____

_____

_____

_____

OBEYING
Changing the Way You Act

How will your thoughts, actions, or reactions change based on today's Scripture reading?

_____

_____

_____

_____

_____

MEMORIZING
God Shaping the Way You Think

Your goal is to memorize one verse every 7 days. What Scripture verse are you memorizing this week? _____

PRAYING
You Speaking To God

Thank You for _____

_____

Forgive me for _____

_____

Help me to _____

_____

Additional prayers or thoughts: _____

_____

_____

Don't forget to use the **Prayer Request Journal** and **Guide to Prayer** in the back of this book.

DAY 13
THE BIBLE READING AND PRAYER JOURNAL

BIBLE READING
God Speaking To You

What Scripture did you read today? _____

What was your favorite verse in today's reading? _____

JOURNALING
Writing Your Thoughts

What is Scripture saying to you about who God is (His character), what He has done (His works), or what He will do (His promises)?

_____

_____

_____

_____

_____

Briefly describe what you learned in your Bible reading today.

_____

_____

_____

_____

_____

OBEYING
Changing the Way You Act

How will your thoughts, actions, or reactions change based on today's Scripture reading?

_____

_____

_____

_____

_____

MEMORIZING
God Shaping the Way You Think

Your goal is to memorize one verse every 7 days. What Scripture verse are you memorizing this week? _____

PRAYING
You Speaking To God

Thank You for _____

_____

Forgive me for _____

_____

Help me to _____

_____

Additional prayers or thoughts: _____

_____

_____

Don't forget to use the **Prayer Request Journal** and **Guide to Prayer** in the back of this book.

DAY 14
THE BIBLE READING AND PRAYER JOURNAL

BIBLE READING
God Speaking To You

What Scripture did you read today? _____

What was your favorite verse in today's reading? _____

JOURNALING
Writing Your Thoughts

What is Scripture saying to you about who God is (His character), what He has done (His works), or what He will do (His promises)?

_____

_____

_____

_____

_____

Briefly describe what you learned in your Bible reading today.

_____

_____

_____

_____

_____

_____

OBEYING
Changing the Way You Act

How will your thoughts, actions, or reactions change based on today's Scripture reading?

_____

_____

_____

_____

_____

MEMORIZING
God Shaping the Way You Think

Your goal is to memorize one verse every 7 days. What Scripture verse are you memorizing this week? _____

PRAYING
You Speaking To God

Thank You for _____

_____

Forgive me for _____

_____

Help me to _____

_____

Additional prayers or thoughts: _____

_____

_____

Don't forget to use the **Prayer Request Journal** and **Guide to Prayer** in the back of this book.

DAY 15
THE BIBLE READING AND PRAYER JOURNAL

BIBLE READING
God Speaking To You

What Scripture did you read today? _____

What was your favorite verse in today's reading? _____

JOURNALING
Writing Your Thoughts

What is Scripture saying to you about who God is (His character), what He has done (His works), or what He will do (His promises)?

_____

_____

_____

_____

_____

Briefly describe what you learned in your Bible reading today.

_____

_____

_____

_____

_____

_____

OBEYING
Changing the Way You Act

How will your thoughts, actions, or reactions change based on today's Scripture reading?

_____

_____

_____

_____

_____

MEMORIZING
God Shaping the Way You Think

Your goal is to memorize one verse every 7 days. What Scripture verse are you memorizing this week? _____

PRAYING
You Speaking To God

Thank You for _____

_____

Forgive me for _____

_____

Help me to _____

_____

Additional prayers or thoughts: _____

_____

_____

Don't forget to use the **Prayer Request Journal** and **Guide to Prayer** in the back of this book.

DAY 16

THE BIBLE READING AND PRAYER JOURNAL

BIBLE READING
God Speaking To You

What Scripture did you read today? _____

What was your favorite verse in today's reading? _____

JOURNALING
Writing Your Thoughts

What is Scripture saying to you about who God is (His character), what He has done (His works), or what He will do (His promises)?

_____

_____

_____

_____

_____

Briefly describe what you learned in your Bible reading today.

_____

_____

_____

_____

_____

_____

OBEYING
Changing the Way You Act

How will your thoughts, actions, or reactions change based on today's Scripture reading?

_____

_____

_____

_____

_____

MEMORIZING
God Shaping the Way You Think

Your goal is to memorize one verse every 7 days. What Scripture verse are you memorizing this week? _____

PRAYING
You Speaking To God

Thank You for _____

_____

Forgive me for _____

_____

Help me to _____

_____

Additional prayers or thoughts: _____

_____

_____

Don't forget to use the **Prayer Request Journal** and **Guide to Prayer** in the back of this book.

DAY 17

THE BIBLE READING AND PRAYER JOURNAL

BIBLE READING
God Speaking To You

What Scripture did you read today? _____

What was your favorite verse in today's reading? _____

JOURNALING
Writing Your Thoughts

What is Scripture saying to you about who God is (His character), what He has done (His works), or what He will do (His promises)?

_____

_____

_____

_____

_____

Briefly describe what you learned in your Bible reading today.

_____

_____

_____

_____

_____

_____

OBEYING
Changing the Way You Act

How will your thoughts, actions, or reactions change based on today's Scripture reading?

_____

_____

_____

_____

_____

MEMORIZING
God Shaping the Way You Think

Your goal is to memorize one verse every 7 days. What Scripture verse are you memorizing this week? _____

PRAYING
You Speaking To God

Thank You for _____

_____

Forgive me for _____

_____

Help me to _____

_____

Additional prayers or thoughts: _____

_____

_____

Don't forget to use the **Prayer Request Journal** and **Guide to Prayer** in the back of this book.

DAY 18
THE BIBLE READING AND PRAYER JOURNAL

BIBLE READING
God Speaking To You

What Scripture did you read today? _____

What was your favorite verse in today's reading? _____

JOURNALING
Writing Your Thoughts

What is Scripture saying to you about who God is (His character), what He has done (His works), or what He will do (His promises)?

_____

_____

_____

_____

_____

Briefly describe what you learned in your Bible reading today.

_____

_____

_____

_____

_____

_____

OBEYING
Changing the Way You Act

How will your thoughts, actions, or reactions change based on today's Scripture reading?

_____

_____

_____

_____

_____

MEMORIZING
God Shaping the Way You Think

Your goal is to memorize one verse every 7 days. What Scripture verse are you memorizing this week? _____

PRAYING
You Speaking To God

Thank You for _____

_____

Forgive me for _____

_____

Help me to _____

_____

Additional prayers or thoughts: _____

_____

_____

Don't forget to use the **Prayer Request Journal** and **Guide to Prayer** in the back of this book.

DAY 19

THE BIBLE READING AND PRAYER JOURNAL

BIBLE READING
God Speaking To You

What Scripture did you read today? _____

What was your favorite verse in today's reading? _____

JOURNALING
Writing Your Thoughts

What is Scripture saying to you about who God is (His character),
what He has done (His works), or what He will do (His promises)?

_____

_____

_____

_____

_____

Briefly describe what you learned in your Bible reading today.

_____

_____

_____

_____

_____

_____

OBEYING
Changing the Way You Act

How will your thoughts, actions, or reactions change based on today's Scripture reading?

_____

_____

_____

_____

_____

MEMORIZING
God Shaping the Way You Think

Your goal is to memorize one verse every 7 days. What Scripture verse are you memorizing this week? _____

PRAYING
You Speaking To God

Thank You for _____

_____

Forgive me for _____

_____

Help me to _____

_____

Additional prayers or thoughts: _____

_____

_____

Don't forget to use the **Prayer Request Journal** and **Guide to Prayer** in the back of this book.

DAY 20

THE BIBLE READING AND PRAYER JOURNAL

BIBLE READING
God Speaking To You

What Scripture did you read today? _____

What was your favorite verse in today's reading? _____

JOURNALING
Writing Your Thoughts

What is Scripture saying to you about who God is (His character),
what He has done (His works), or what He will do (His promises)?

_____

_____

_____

_____

_____

Briefly describe what you learned in your Bible reading today.

_____

_____

_____

_____

_____

_____

OBEYING
Changing the Way You Act

How will your thoughts, actions, or reactions change based on today's Scripture reading?

_____

_____

_____

_____

_____

MEMORIZING
God Shaping the Way You Think

Your goal is to memorize one verse every 7 days. What Scripture verse are you memorizing this week? _____

PRAYING
You Speaking To God

Thank You for _____

_____

Forgive me for _____

_____

Help me to _____

_____

Additional prayers or thoughts: _____

_____

_____

Don't forget to use the **Prayer Request Journal** and **Guide to Prayer** in the back of this book.

DAY 21
THE BIBLE READING AND PRAYER JOURNAL

BIBLE READING
God Speaking To You

What Scripture did you read today? _____

What was your favorite verse in today's reading? _____

JOURNALING
Writing Your Thoughts

What is Scripture saying to you about who God is (His character), what He has done (His works), or what He will do (His promises)?

_____

_____

_____

_____

_____

Briefly describe what you learned in your Bible reading today.

_____

_____

_____

_____

_____

_____

OBEYING
Changing the Way You Act

How will your thoughts, actions, or reactions change based on today's Scripture reading?

_____

_____

_____

_____

_____

MEMORIZING
God Shaping the Way You Think

Your goal is to memorize one verse every 7 days. What Scripture verse are you memorizing this week? _____

PRAYING
You Speaking To God

Thank You for _____

_____

Forgive me for _____

_____

Help me to _____

_____

Additional prayers or thoughts: _____

_____

_____

Don't forget to use the **Prayer Request Journal** and **Guide to Prayer** in the back of this book.

DAY 22

THE BIBLE READING AND PRAYER JOURNAL

BIBLE READING
God Speaking To You

What Scripture did you read today? _____

What was your favorite verse in today's reading? _____

JOURNALING
Writing Your Thoughts

What is Scripture saying to you about who God is (His character), what He has done (His works), or what He will do (His promises)?

_____

_____

_____

_____

_____

Briefly describe what you learned in your Bible reading today.

_____

_____

_____

_____

_____

_____

OBEYING
Changing the Way You Act

How will your thoughts, actions, or reactions change based on today's Scripture reading?

_____

_____

_____

_____

_____

MEMORIZING
God Shaping the Way You Think

Your goal is to memorize one verse every 7 days. What Scripture verse are you memorizing this week? _____

PRAYING
You Speaking To God

Thank You for _____

_____

Forgive me for _____

_____

Help me to _____

_____

Additional prayers or thoughts: _____

_____

_____

Don't forget to use the **Prayer Request Journal** and **Guide to Prayer** in the back of this book.

DAY 23
THE BIBLE READING AND PRAYER JOURNAL

BIBLE READING
God Speaking To You

What Scripture did you read today? _____

What was your favorite verse in today's reading? _____

JOURNALING
Writing Your Thoughts

What is Scripture saying to you about who God is (His character), what He has done (His works), or what He will do (His promises)?

_____

_____

_____

_____

_____

Briefly describe what you learned in your Bible reading today.

_____

_____

_____

_____

_____

_____

OBEYING
Changing the Way You Act

How will your thoughts, actions, or reactions change based on today's Scripture reading?

_____

_____

_____

_____

_____

MEMORIZING
God Shaping the Way You Think

Your goal is to memorize one verse every 7 days. What Scripture verse are you memorizing this week? _____

PRAYING
You Speaking To God

Thank You for _____

_____

Forgive me for _____

_____

Help me to _____

_____

Additional prayers or thoughts: _____

_____

_____

Don't forget to use the **Prayer Request Journal** and **Guide to Prayer** in the back of this book.

DAY 24
THE BIBLE READING AND PRAYER JOURNAL

BIBLE READING
God Speaking To You

What Scripture did you read today? _____

What was your favorite verse in today's reading? _____

JOURNALING
Writing Your Thoughts

What is Scripture saying to you about who God is (His character), what He has done (His works), or what He will do (His promises)?

_____

_____

_____

_____

_____

Briefly describe what you learned in your Bible reading today.

_____

_____

_____

_____

_____

_____

OBEYING
Changing the Way You Act

How will your thoughts, actions, or reactions change based on today's Scripture reading?

_____

_____

_____

_____

_____

MEMORIZING
God Shaping the Way You Think

Your goal is to memorize one verse every 7 days. What Scripture verse are you memorizing this week? _____

PRAYING
You Speaking To God

Thank You for _____

_____

Forgive me for _____

_____

Help me to _____

_____

Additional prayers or thoughts: _____

_____

_____

Don't forget to use the **Prayer Request Journal** and **Guide to Prayer** in the back of this book.

DAY 25
THE BIBLE READING AND PRAYER JOURNAL

BIBLE READING
God Speaking To You

What Scripture did you read today? _____

What was your favorite verse in today's reading? _____

JOURNALING
Writing Your Thoughts

What is Scripture saying to you about who God is (His character), what He has done (His works), or what He will do (His promises)?

_____

_____

_____

_____

_____

Briefly describe what you learned in your Bible reading today.

_____

_____

_____

_____

_____

_____

OBEYING
Changing the Way You Act

How will your thoughts, actions, or reactions change based on today's Scripture reading?

_____

_____

_____

_____

_____

MEMORIZING
God Shaping the Way You Think

Your goal is to memorize one verse every 7 days. What Scripture verse are you memorizing this week? _____

PRAYING
You Speaking To God

Thank You for _____

_____

Forgive me for _____

_____

Help me to _____

_____

Additional prayers or thoughts: _____

_____

_____

Don't forget to use the **Prayer Request Journal** and **Guide to Prayer** in the back of this book.

DAY 26

THE BIBLE READING AND PRAYER JOURNAL

BIBLE READING
God Speaking To You

What Scripture did you read today? _____

What was your favorite verse in today's reading? _____

JOURNALING
Writing Your Thoughts

What is Scripture saying to you about who God is (His character), what He has done (His works), or what He will do (His promises)?

_____

_____

_____

_____

Briefly describe what you learned in your Bible reading today.

_____

_____

_____

_____

_____

_____

OBEYING
Changing the Way You Act

How will your thoughts, actions, or reactions change based on today's Scripture reading?

_____

_____

_____

_____

_____

MEMORIZING
God Shaping the Way You Think

Your goal is to memorize one verse every 7 days. What Scripture verse are you memorizing this week? _____

PRAYING
You Speaking To God

Thank You for _____

_____

Forgive me for _____

_____

Help me to _____

_____

Additional prayers or thoughts: _____

_____

_____

Don't forget to use the **Prayer Request Journal** and **Guide to Prayer** in the back of this book.

DAY 27
THE BIBLE READING AND PRAYER JOURNAL

BIBLE READING
God Speaking To You

What Scripture did you read today? _____

What was your favorite verse in today's reading? _____

JOURNALING
Writing Your Thoughts

What is Scripture saying to you about who God is (His character), what He has done (His works), or what He will do (His promises)?

_____

_____

_____

_____

_____

Briefly describe what you learned in your Bible reading today.

_____

_____

_____

_____

_____

_____

OBEYING
Changing the Way You Act

How will your thoughts, actions, or reactions change based on today's Scripture reading?

_____

_____

_____

_____

_____

MEMORIZING
God Shaping the Way You Think

Your goal is to memorize one verse every 7 days. What Scripture verse are you memorizing this week? _____

PRAYING
You Speaking To God

Thank You for _____

_____

Forgive me for _____

_____

Help me to _____

_____

Additional prayers or thoughts: _____

_____

_____

Don't forget to use the **Prayer Request Journal** and **Guide to Prayer** in the back of this book.

DAY 28

BIBLE READING
God Speaking To You

What Scripture did you read today? _____

What was your favorite verse in today's reading? _____

JOURNALING
Writing Your Thoughts

What is Scripture saying to you about who God is (His character), what He has done (His works), or what He will do (His promises)?

_____

_____

_____

_____

_____

Briefly describe what you learned in your Bible reading today.

_____

_____

_____

_____

_____

_____

OBEYING
Changing the Way You Act

How will your thoughts, actions, or reactions change based on today's Scripture reading?

_____

_____

_____

_____

_____

MEMORIZING
God Shaping the Way You Think

Your goal is to memorize one verse every 7 days. What Scripture verse are you memorizing this week? _____

PRAYING
You Speaking To God

Thank You for _____

_____

Forgive me for _____

_____

Help me to _____

_____

Additional prayers or thoughts: _____

_____

_____

Don't forget to use the **Prayer Request Journal** and **Guide to Prayer** in the back of this book.

DAY 29

BIBLE READING
God Speaking To You

What Scripture did you read today? _____

What was your favorite verse in today's reading? _____

JOURNALING
Writing Your Thoughts

What is Scripture saying to you about who God is (His character), what He has done (His works), or what He will do (His promises)?

_____

_____

_____

_____

_____

Briefly describe what you learned in your Bible reading today.

_____

_____

_____

_____

_____

_____

OBEYING
Changing the Way You Act

How will your thoughts, actions, or reactions change based on today's Scripture reading?

_____

_____

_____

_____

_____

MEMORIZING
God Shaping the Way You Think

Your goal is to memorize one verse every 7 days. What Scripture verse are you memorizing this week? _____

PRAYING
You Speaking To God

Thank You for _____

_____

Forgive me for _____

_____

Help me to _____

_____

Additional prayers or thoughts: _____

_____

_____

Don't forget to use the **Prayer Request Journal** and **Guide to Prayer** in the back of this book.

DAY 30

THE BIBLE READING AND PRAYER JOURNAL

BIBLE READING
God Speaking To You

What Scripture did you read today? _____

What was your favorite verse in today's reading? _____

JOURNALING
Writing Your Thoughts

What is Scripture saying to you about who God is (His character), what He has done (His works), or what He will do (His promises)?

_____

_____

_____

_____

_____

Briefly describe what you learned in your Bible reading today.

_____

_____

_____

_____

_____

_____

OBEYING
Changing the Way You Act

How will your thoughts, actions, or reactions change based on today's Scripture reading?

_____

_____

_____

_____

_____

MEMORIZING
God Shaping the Way You Think

Your goal is to memorize one verse every 7 days. What Scripture verse are you memorizing this week? _____

PRAYING
You Speaking To God

Thank You for _____

_____

Forgive me for _____

_____

Help me to _____

_____

Additional prayers or thoughts: _____

_____

_____

Don't forget to use the **Prayer Request Journal** and **Guide to Prayer** in the back of this book.

DAY 31

THE BIBLE READING AND PRAYER JOURNAL

BIBLE READING
God Speaking To You

What Scripture did you read today? _____

What was your favorite verse in today's reading? _____

JOURNALING
Writing Your Thoughts

What is Scripture saying to you about who God is (His character),
what He has done (His works), or what He will do (His promises)?

_____

_____

_____

_____

_____

Briefly describe what you learned in your Bible reading today.

_____

_____

_____

_____

_____

_____

OBEYING
Changing the Way You Act

How will your thoughts, actions, or reactions change based on today's Scripture reading?

_____

_____

_____

_____

_____

MEMORIZING
God Shaping the Way You Think

Your goal is to memorize one verse every 7 days. What Scripture verse are you memorizing this week? _____

PRAYING
You Speaking To God

Thank You for _____

_____

Forgive me for _____

_____

Help me to _____

_____

Additional prayers or thoughts: _____

_____

_____

Don't forget to use the **Prayer Request Journal** and **Guide to Prayer** in the back of this book.

DAY 32

THE BIBLE READING AND PRAYER JOURNAL

BIBLE READING
God Speaking To You

What Scripture did you read today? _____

What was your favorite verse in today's reading? _____

JOURNALING
Writing Your Thoughts

What is Scripture saying to you about who God is (His character), what He has done (His works), or what He will do (His promises)?

_____

_____

_____

_____

_____

Briefly describe what you learned in your Bible reading today.

_____

_____

_____

_____

_____

_____

OBEYING
Changing the Way You Act

How will your thoughts, actions, or reactions change based on today's Scripture reading?

_____

_____

_____

_____

_____

MEMORIZING
God Shaping the Way You Think

Your goal is to memorize one verse every 7 days. What Scripture verse are you memorizing this week? _____

PRAYING
You Speaking To God

Thank You for _____

_____

Forgive me for _____

_____

Help me to _____

_____

Additional prayers or thoughts: _____

_____

_____

Don't forget to use the **Prayer Request Journal** and **Guide to Prayer** in the back of this book.

DAY 33
THE BIBLE READING AND PRAYER JOURNAL

BIBLE READING
God Speaking To You

What Scripture did you read today? _____

What was your favorite verse in today's reading? _____

JOURNALING
Writing Your Thoughts

What is Scripture saying to you about who God is (His character), what He has done (His works), or what He will do (His promises)?

_____

_____

_____

_____

_____

Briefly describe what you learned in your Bible reading today.

_____

_____

_____

_____

_____

_____

OBEYING
Changing the Way You Act

How will your thoughts, actions, or reactions change based on today's Scripture reading?

_____

_____

_____

_____

_____

MEMORIZING
God Shaping the Way You Think

Your goal is to memorize one verse every 7 days. What Scripture verse are you memorizing this week? _____

PRAYING
You Speaking To God

Thank You for _____

_____

Forgive me for _____

_____

Help me to _____

_____

Additional prayers or thoughts: _____

_____

_____

Don't forget to use the **Prayer Request Journal** and **Guide to Prayer** in the back of this book.

DAY 34

THE BIBLE READING AND PRAYER JOURNAL

BIBLE READING
God Speaking To You

What Scripture did you read today? _____

What was your favorite verse in today's reading? _____

JOURNALING
Writing Your Thoughts

What is Scripture saying to you about who God is (His character), what He has done (His works), or what He will do (His promises)?

_____

_____

_____

_____

_____

Briefly describe what you learned in your Bible reading today.

_____

_____

_____

_____

_____

_____

OBEYING
Changing the Way You Act

How will your thoughts, actions, or reactions change based on today's Scripture reading?

_____

_____

_____

_____

_____

MEMORIZING
God Shaping the Way You Think

Your goal is to memorize one verse every 7 days. What Scripture verse are you memorizing this week? _____

PRAYING
You Speaking To God

Thank You for _____

_____

Forgive me for _____

_____

Help me to _____

_____

Additional prayers or thoughts: _____

_____

_____

Don't forget to use the **Prayer Request Journal** and **Guide to Prayer** in the back of this book.

DAY 35

THE BIBLE READING AND PRAYER JOURNAL

BIBLE READING
God Speaking To You

What Scripture did you read today? _____

What was your favorite verse in today's reading? _____

JOURNALING
Writing Your Thoughts

What is Scripture saying to you about who God is (His character), what He has done (His works), or what He will do (His promises)?

_____

_____

_____

_____

_____

Briefly describe what you learned in your Bible reading today.

_____

_____

_____

_____

_____

_____

OBEYING
Changing the Way You Act

How will your thoughts, actions, or reactions change based on today's Scripture reading?

_____

_____

_____

_____

_____

MEMORIZING
God Shaping the Way You Think

Your goal is to memorize one verse every 7 days. What Scripture verse are you memorizing this week? _____

PRAYING
You Speaking To God

Thank You for _____

_____

Forgive me for _____

_____

Help me to _____

_____

Additional prayers or thoughts: _____

_____

_____

Don't forget to use the **Prayer Request Journal** and **Guide to Prayer** in the back of this book.

DAY 36
THE BIBLE READING AND PRAYER JOURNAL

BIBLE READING
God Speaking To You

What Scripture did you read today? _____

What was your favorite verse in today's reading? _____

JOURNALING
Writing Your Thoughts

What is Scripture saying to you about who God is (His character), what He has done (His works), or what He will do (His promises)?

_____

_____

_____

_____

_____

Briefly describe what you learned in your Bible reading today.

_____

_____

_____

_____

_____

_____

OBEYING
Changing the Way You Act

How will your thoughts, actions, or reactions change based on today's Scripture reading?

_____

_____

_____

_____

_____

MEMORIZING
God Shaping the Way You Think

Your goal is to memorize one verse every 7 days. What Scripture verse are you memorizing this week? _____

PRAYING
You Speaking To God

Thank You for _____

_____

Forgive me for _____

_____

Help me to _____

_____

Additional prayers or thoughts: _____

_____

_____

Don't forget to use the **Prayer Request Journal** and **Guide to Prayer** in the back of this book.

DAY 37
THE BIBLE READING AND PRAYER JOURNAL

BIBLE READING
God Speaking To You

What Scripture did you read today? _____

What was your favorite verse in today's reading? _____

JOURNALING
Writing Your Thoughts

What is Scripture saying to you about who God is (His character), what He has done (His works), or what He will do (His promises)?

_____

_____

_____

_____

_____

Briefly describe what you learned in your Bible reading today.

_____

_____

_____

_____

_____

_____

OBEYING
Changing the Way You Act

How will your thoughts, actions, or reactions change based on today's Scripture reading?

_____

_____

_____

_____

_____

MEMORIZING
God Shaping the Way You Think

Your goal is to memorize one verse every 7 days. What Scripture verse are you memorizing this week? _____

PRAYING
You Speaking To God

Thank You for _____

_____

Forgive me for _____

_____

Help me to _____

_____

Additional prayers or thoughts: _____

_____

_____

Don't forget to use the **Prayer Request Journal** and **Guide to Prayer** in the back of this book.

95

DAY 38

THE BIBLE READING AND PRAYER JOURNAL

BIBLE READING
God Speaking To You

What Scripture did you read today? _____

What was your favorite verse in today's reading? _____

JOURNALING
Writing Your Thoughts

What is Scripture saying to you about who God is (His character), what He has done (His works), or what He will do (His promises)?

_____

_____

_____

_____

_____

Briefly describe what you learned in your Bible reading today.

_____

_____

_____

_____

_____

_____

OBEYING
Changing the Way You Act

How will your thoughts, actions, or reactions change based on today's Scripture reading?

_____

_____

_____

_____

_____

MEMORIZING
God Shaping the Way You Think

Your goal is to memorize one verse every 7 days. What Scripture verse are you memorizing this week? _____

PRAYING
You Speaking To God

Thank You for _____

_____

Forgive me for _____

_____

Help me to _____

_____

Additional prayers or thoughts: _____

_____

_____

Don't forget to use the **Prayer Request Journal** and **Guide to Prayer** in the back of this book.

DAY 39
THE BIBLE READING AND PRAYER JOURNAL

BIBLE READING
God Speaking To You

What Scripture did you read today? _____

What was your favorite verse in today's reading? _____

JOURNALING
Writing Your Thoughts

What is Scripture saying to you about who God is (His character), what He has done (His works), or what He will do (His promises)?

_____

_____

_____

_____

_____

Briefly describe what you learned in your Bible reading today.

_____

_____

_____

_____

_____

_____

OBEYING
Changing the Way You Act

How will your thoughts, actions, or reactions change based on today's Scripture reading?

_____

_____

_____

_____

_____

MEMORIZING
God Shaping the Way You Think

Your goal is to memorize one verse every 7 days. What Scripture verse are you memorizing this week? _____

PRAYING
You Speaking To God

Thank You for _____

_____

Forgive me for _____

_____

Help me to _____

_____

Additional prayers or thoughts: _____

_____

_____

Don't forget to use the **Prayer Request Journal** and **Guide to Prayer** in the back of this book.

DAY 40

THE BIBLE READING AND PRAYER JOURNAL

BIBLE READING
God Speaking To You

What Scripture did you read today? _____

What was your favorite verse in today's reading? _____

JOURNALING
Writing Your Thoughts

What is Scripture saying to you about who God is (His character), what He has done (His works), or what He will do (His promises)?

_____

_____

_____

_____

_____

Briefly describe what you learned in your Bible reading today.

_____

_____

_____

_____

_____

_____

OBEYING
Changing the Way You Act

How will your thoughts, actions, or reactions change based on today's Scripture reading?

_____

_____

_____

_____

_____

MEMORIZING
God Shaping the Way You Think

Your goal is to memorize one verse every 7 days. What Scripture verse are you memorizing this week? _____

PRAYING
You Speaking To God

Thank You for _____

_____

Forgive me for _____

_____

Help me to _____

_____

Additional prayers or thoughts: _____

_____

_____

Don't forget to use the **Prayer Request Journal** and **Guide to Prayer** in the back of this book.

SERMON NOTES 1

LISTENING TO ONE SERMON A WEEK

SERMON INFORMATION

Speaker: _____

Date: _____

SERMON NOTES

_____
_____
_____
_____
_____
_____
_____
_____
_____
_____
_____
_____
_____

SERMON APPLICATION

_____
_____
_____

SERMON NOTES 2

LISTENING TO ONE SERMON A WEEK

SERMON INFORMATION

Speaker: _____

Date: _____

SERMON NOTES

_____

_____

_____

_____

_____

_____

_____

_____

_____

_____

_____

_____

_____

_____

SERMON APPLICATION

_____

_____

_____

SERMON NOTES 3
LISTENING TO ONE SERMON A WEEK

SERMON INFORMATION

Speaker: _____

Date: _____

SERMON NOTES

_____
_____
_____
_____
_____
_____
_____
_____
_____
_____
_____
_____
_____

SERMON APPLICATION

_____
_____
_____

SERMON NOTES 4
LISTENING TO ONE SERMON A WEEK

SERMON INFORMATION

Speaker: _____

Date: _____

SERMON NOTES

_____
_____
_____
_____
_____
_____
_____
_____
_____
_____
_____
_____
_____
_____
_____
_____

SERMON APPLICATION

_____
_____
_____

SERMON NOTES 5

LISTENING TO ONE SERMON A WEEK

SERMON INFORMATION

Speaker: _____

Date: _____

SERMON NOTES

_____
_____
_____
_____
_____
_____
_____
_____
_____
_____
_____
_____
_____

SERMON APPLICATION

_____
_____
_____

SERMON NOTES 6
LISTENING TO ONE SERMON A WEEK

SERMON INFORMATION

Speaker: _____

Date: _____

SERMON NOTES

_____
_____
_____
_____
_____
_____
_____
_____
_____
_____
_____
_____
_____
_____

SERMON APPLICATION

_____
_____
_____

BIBLE READING RESOURCE LIST

BIBLE STUDY RESOURCES

Bible.org – A web-based resource where nearly 60,000 people visit each day in order to help prepare lessons or find answers to spiritual questions.

Bible Hub (biblehub.com)- Features topical, Greek (language of the New Testament) and Hebrew (language of the Old Testament) study tools, plus concordances (listing of words found in the Bible and the places where they are used), commentaries (books that help explain the meaning of the Bible), dictionaries, sermons, and devotionals.

Crosswalk (crosswalk.com) – A site centered on helping people grow in their faith by providing resources such as devotionals, family-oriented discussions, cultural thoughts, and more.

Got Questions (gotquestions.org) – This site or app is an extensive resource to "provide Biblical answers to life's various questions." If you have a question about anything faith related, this site is likely to have the answer.

YouVersion (bible.com) - A free Bible on your phone, tablet, and computer. YouVersion is a simple, ad-free Bible that brings God's Word into your daily life.

DEFENDING FAITH RESOURCES

Answers in Genesis - An apologetics ministry dedicated to helping Christians defend their faith and proclaim the gospel of Jesus Christ effectively. They focus on providing answers to questions about the Bible—particularly the book of Genesis—regarding key issues such as creation, evolution, science, and the age of the earth.

Christian Apologetics & Research Ministry (carm.org) – A Christian ministry dedicated to the promotion and defense of the Gospel, doctrine, and theology. CARM analyzes religious and non-religious movements and compares them to the Bible.

STUDY BIBLE RESOURCES (Bibles with explanation notes)
ESV Study Bible; Life Application Study Bible; MacArthur Study Bible

SPIRITUAL DISCIPLINES RESOURCES
Solid Joys Daily Bible Devotional (solidjoys.desiringgod.org) – Read daily devotionals online or download the app

Wisdom Hunters (wisdomhunters.com) – Available online or as an app, this daily devotional will help you discover inspiration and resources needed to encourage wise living and decision-making.

YouVersion Plans (bible.com/reading-plans) – There are dozens of Bible reading plans in the YouVersion app or on the website.

TERMS AND TYPES OF BIBLE RESOURCES
Commentaries - books that help explain the meaning of the Bible (Bible Knowledge Commentary, The Bible Exposition Commentary)

Concordances - listing of words found in the Bible and the places where they are used

Cross References - verse with a related theme/topic as the verse being read

Devotionals - book that provide a plan to read the Bible and explanation of what is being read

BIBLE READING PLANS

Some people have a difficult time knowing what to read, so here are a couple of Bible reading plans. All of these will not be exactly 40 days, but you can modify them along the way to fit your reading schedule.

MARK BIBLE READING PLAN (39 READINGS)

Mark 1:1-11
Mark 1:12-20
Mark 1:21-35
Mark 1:36-Mark 2:12
Mark 2:13-17
Mark 2:18-22
Mark 2:23-Mark 3:12
Mark 3:13-35
Mark 4:1-20
Mark 4:21-34
Mark 4:35-Mark 5:43
Mark 6:1-13, 30-31
Mark 6:14-29
Mark 6:32-44
Mark 6:45-56
Mark 7:1-23
Mark 7:24-37
Mark 8:1-21
Mark 8:22-33
Mark 8:34-38

Mark 9:1-13
Mark 9:14-29
Mark 9:30-50
Mark 10:1-31
Mark 10:32-52
Mark 11:1-11, 15-19
Mark 11:12-14, 20-33
Mark 12:1-12
Mark 12:13-17
Mark 12:18-34
Mark 12:35-44
Mark 13:1-37
Mark 14:1-11
Mark 14:12-25
Mark 14:26-42
Mark 14:43-72
Mark 15:1-23
Mark 15:24-47
Mark 16:1-20

ACTS BIBLE READING PLAN (35 READINGS)

Acts 1:1-8
Acts 1:9-26
Acts 2:1-39
Acts 2:40-47
Acts 3:1-26
Acts 4:1-31
Acts 4:32-Acts 5:11
Acts 5:12-42
Acts 6:1-15
Acts 7:1-60
Acts 8:1-24
Acts 8:25-40
Acts 9:1-19
Acts 9:20-31
Acts 9:32-43
Acts 10:1-16
Acts 10:17-48
Acts 11:1-18

Acts 11:19-26
Acts 11:27-Acts 12:24
Acts 12:25-Acts 13:41
Acts 13:42-Acts 14:28
Acts 15:1-29
Acts 15:30-Acts 16:15
Acts 16:16-40
Acts 17:1-34
Acts 18:1-28
Acts 19:1-Acts 20:24
Acts 20:25-Acts 21:36
Acts 21:37-Acts 22:29
Acts 22:30-Acts 23:35
Acts 24:1-27
Acts 25:1-Acts 26:32
Acts 27:1-44
Acts 28:1-31

JAMES BIBLE READING PLAN (12 READINGS)

James 1:1-8
James 1:9-18
James 1:19-27
James 2:1-13
James 2:14-26
James 3:1-12

James 3:13-18
James 4:1-12
James 4:13-17
James 5:1-6
James 5:7-12
James 5:13-20

1-3 JOHN AND JUDE (15 READINGS)

1 John 1:1-4; 2:12-14

1 John 1:5-1 John 2:2

1 John 2:3-11

1 John 2:15-17

1 John 2:28-1 John 3:3

1 John 3:4-10

1 John 3:11-23

1 John 3:24-1 John 4:6

1 John 4:7-21

1 John 5:1-12

1 John 5:13-21

2 John 1-13

3 John 1-14

Jude 1-11

Jude 12-25

SUGGESTED VERSES TO MEMORIZE

The Bible has so many wonderful verses and I am a proponent of committing some of them to memory. I believe that memorizing Scripture has the ability to shape a person's mind and help them focus on truth. The following verses are some of my personal favorites.

Genesis 1:1 (Creation)

Genesis 1:26 (Man created in the image of God)

Genesis 3:15 (First Gospel given after man's sin)

Genesis 15:6 (Abram believed God and became righteous)

Joshua 1:9 (Reading and obeying God's Word brings success)

1 Samuel 16:7 (God looks on the heart, not the outward appearance)

Psalms 1:1-2 (Delighting in God's Word)

Psalms 37:4 (Delight in God)

Proverbs 3:5-6 (Trust in the Lord)

Isaiah 9:6 (A Savior Promised)

Isaiah 40:26 (Character of God)

Lamentations 3:22-23 (God's mercies are new every morning)

Matthew 1:21 (Jesus will save people from their sin)

John 3:16-17 (God's love and salvation)

John 14:6 (Jesus is the only way to God)

Romans 3:23 (All have sinned)

Romans 6:23 (God's gift is eternal life)

Romans 8:28 (God works everything together for good)

Romans 8:38-39 (Nothing can separate us from the love of God)

2 Corinthians 12:9 (God's strength made perfect in weakness)

Ephesians 2:8-9 (We are saved by grace through faith)

Hebrews 12:6 (God rewards those who seek Him)

James 1:22 (Be doers of the Word)

2 Peter 3:9 (God is patient)

1 John 3:18 (Love in deed and truth)

Revelation 21:4 (God wipes away every tear and makes all things new)

PRAYERS OF SUBMISSION

Submit my *mind* (guard what I think)

Psalm 139:23 (ESV) Search me, O God, and know my heart! Try me and know my thoughts! **24** And see if there be any grievous way in me, and lead me in the way everlasting!

Submit my *eyes* (guard what I see)

Psalm 101:3 (ESV) I will not set before my eyes anything that is worthless. I hate the work of those who fall away; it shall not cling to me.

Submit my *ears* (guard what I listen to)

Psalm 1:1 (ESV) Blessed is the man who walks not in the counsel of the wicked, nor stands in the way of sinners, nor sits in the seat of scoffers; **2** but his delight is in the law of the Lord, and on his law he meditates day and night.

Submit my *mouth* (guard what I say)

Psalm 19:14 (ESV) Let the words of my mouth and the meditation of my heart be acceptable in your sight, O Lord, my rock and my redeemer.

Submit my *hands* (guide my actions)

1 Corinthians 10:31 (ESV) So, whether you eat or drink, or whatever you do, do all to the glory of God.

Submit my *heart* (guide what I desire)

Proverbs 4:23 (ESV) Keep your heart with all vigilance, for from it flow the springs of life.

Submit my *feet* (guide the direction of my life)

Ephesians 2:10 (ESV) For we are his workmanship, created in Christ Jesus for good works, which God prepared beforehand, that we should walk in them.

PRAYERS OF FILLING

Fill me with the *Holy Spirit of God*

Ephesians 5:18 (ESV) And do not get drunk with wine, for that is debauchery, but be filled with the Spirit, **19** addressing one another in psalms and hymns and spiritual songs, singing and making melody to the Lord with your heart, **20** giving thanks always and for everything to God the Father in the name of our Lord Jesus Christ…

Fill me with the *Love of God*

1 John 3:18 (ESV) Little children, let us not love in word or talk but in deed and in truth.

Fill me with the *Word of God*

Colossians 3:16 (ESV) Let the word of Christ dwell in you richly…

Fill me with the *Wisdom of God*

James 1:5 (ESV) If any of you lacks wisdom, let him ask God, who gives generously to all without reproach, and it will be given him.

PRAYERS OF CONFESSION AND RENEWAL

Confess my sin

1 John 1:9 (ESV) If we confess our sins, he is faithful and just to forgive us our sins and to cleanse us from all unrighteousness.

Forsake my sin

Proverbs 28:13 (ESV) Whoever conceals his transgressions will not prosper, but he who confesses and forsakes them will obtain mercy.

Remove my sin

Psalm 103:12 (ESV) …as far as the east is from the west, so far does he remove our transgressions from us.

Renew me

Psalm 51:10 (ESV) Create in me a clean heart, O God, and renew a right spirit within me.

PRAYERS OF FAITH

Pray in secret and God will reward you openly

Matthew 6:5 (ESV) And when you pray, you must not be like the hypocrites. For they love to stand and pray in the synagogues and at the street corners, that they may be seen by others. Truly, I say to you, they have received their reward. **6** But when you pray, go into your room and shut the door and pray to your Father who is in secret. And your Father who sees in secret will reward you.

God gives good things to those who ask

Matthew 7:7 (ESV) Ask, and it will be given to you; seek, and you will find; knock, and it will be opened to you. **8** For everyone who asks receives, and the one who seeks finds, and to the one who knocks it will be opened. **9** Or which one of you, if his son asks him for bread, will give him a stone? **10** Or if he asks for a fish, will give him a serpent? **11** If you then, who are evil, know how to give good gifts to your children, how much more will your Father who is in heaven give good things to those who ask him!

Small faith in God's power accomplishes the impossible

Matthew 17:20 (ESV) ...For truly, I say to you, if you have faith like a grain of mustard seed, you will say to this mountain, 'Move from here to there,' and it will move, and nothing will be impossible for you."

What you ask in prayer, believing, will be received

Matthew 21:21 (ESV) And Jesus answered them, "Truly, I say to you, if you have faith and do not doubt, you will not only do what has been done to the fig tree, but even if you say to this mountain, 'Be taken up and thrown into the sea,' it will happen. **22** And whatever you ask in prayer, you will receive, if you have faith."

Weak faith is understood by God and strong faith is gained through prayer

Mark 9:23 (ESV) And Jesus said to him, "'If you can'! All things are possible for one who believes." **24** Immediately the father of the child cried out and said, "I believe; help my unbelief!" **28** And when he had entered the house, his disciples asked him privately, "Why could we not cast it out?" **29** And he said to them, "This kind cannot be driven out by anything but prayer."

Believe and you will receive

Mark 11:23 (ESV) Truly, I say to you, whoever says to this mountain, "Be taken up and thrown into the sea," and does not doubt in his heart, but believes that what he says will come to pass, it will be done for him. **24** Therefore I tell you, whatever you ask in prayer, believe that you have received it, and it will be yours.

Anything asked in the name of Jesus will be done

John 14:12 (ESV) …whoever believes in me will also do the works that I do; and greater works than these will he do, because I am going to the Father. **13** Whatever you ask in my name, this I will do, that the Father may be glorified in the Son. **14** If you ask me anything in my name, I will do it.

When we ask according to God's will, He always gives what we have requested

1 John 5:14 (ESV) And this is the confidence that we have toward him, that if we ask anything according to his will he hears us. **15** And if we know that he hears us in whatever we ask, we know that we have the requests that we have asked of him.

PRAYERS OF GOD'S WILL

Be satisfied in God and He will grant the desires of your heart

Psalm 37:4 (ESV) Delight yourself in the Lord, and he will give you the desires of your heart. **5** Commit your way to the Lord; trust in him, and he will act.

God gives good things to those who walk in holiness

Psalm 84:11 (ESV) For the Lord God is a sun and shield; the Lord bestows favor and honor. No good thing does he withhold from those who walk uprightly.

God desires all men to be saved

1 Timothy 2:3 (ESV) This is good, and it is pleasing in the sight of God our Savior, **4** who desires all people to be saved and to come to the knowledge of the truth.

God is not willing that any man should die, but that all should repent

2 Peter 3:9 (ESV) The Lord is not slow to fulfill his promise as some count slowness, but is patient toward you, not wishing that any should perish, but that all should reach repentance.

PRAYER REQUEST JOURNAL

Request Date	Request Details	Answer Date

Request Date	Request Details	Answer Date

WHAT'S NEXT?

I would like to personally thank you for taking the last 40 days to spend personal time with God. If you are reading this, my prayer is that you have been challenged in your faith journey and are able to look back on these 40 days to see tangible life change. My hope is that you have also established a habit of reading God's Word. Habits can be good things and I believe listening to God consistently is one of the best disciplines you can develop.

Along with my hope for life change and the establishment of good habits, I am also hopeful for you to continue. Tomorrow is probably the most critical day in this journey because it will be the first day in 40 days that you may not have a plan. In my own life, having a plan for listening to God keeps me on track. If I do not have a plan, I typically get out of the habit of reading God's Word. Since you are already in the habit, can I challenge you to have a plan?

Here are some immediate ways you can continue reading God's Word.

- **Download the YouVersion app** and find a Bible reading plan to begin tomorrow. They have hundreds of plans to fit any schedule or time of life.
- **Purchase one of my other books** to keep you connected with God. I have written several books that take you through a book of the Bible. It has been my passion to help people interact with God on a daily basis. You can visit tomhogsed.co to find all of the current titles available or visit my author page on Amazon at amazon.com/author/tomhogsed.
- **Repurchasing this book** may be a way to continue the journey you've started. If this resource has kept you on track, consider adding another journaling book to build spiritual milestones.

THE FIRST TWO STEPS TO BEGIN YOUR FAITH JOURNEY

STEP 1: FAITH AND FORGIVENESS

Although this book may be an important resource, no one can fully understand God's plan until they have started a relationship with Him and experienced His forgiveness. How does a person know if they have a relationship with God and have been forgiven by Him? I'm glad you asked.

At the beginning of human history, God created Adam and Eve (Genesis 1:26; Genesis 2:8-25) and placed them into the Garden of Eden where they enjoyed perfect companionship with Him. They were given freedom in the garden to eat of any tree except the tree of the knowledge of good and evil (Genesis 2:15-17). If they disobeyed God's commandment and ate from the tree, they would experience physical death and eternal separation from God (Genesis 2:17). After listening to the lies of Satan (a fallen angel), Eve and eventually Adam disregarded God's commandment by eating from the forbidden tree (Genesis 3:1-13) and their disobedience brought the consequence of sin, death, and eternal separation from God upon the entire human race (Romans 5:12).

Much like Adam and Eve, you have sinned by disobeying God's commandments. Even the person who thinks of himself as good and moral has broken God's law (Romans 3:10-12) by doing things such as dishonoring their parents, hating, lusting, stealing, and lying.

Before you begin weighing your good works and your bad works, remember that Adam and Eve were sentenced to death because of a single act of rebellion; therefore, if you have only sinned once, you are guilty before a holy and righteous God (James 2:10). Whether your sins are many or few, you must be punished for sin through death and eternal separation from God (Romans 6:23). Good works cannot satisfy God's prescribed punishment for sin. "For the wages of sin is death...." (Romans 6:23, NKJV).

Is there any hope of forgiveness for those who have sinned? Because Adam and Eve disobeyed, God promised that from the woman's seed (offspring) He would eventually bring into the world a Savior to defeat the works of Satan and destroy sin and death (Genesis 3:15). How would this be accomplished? This Savior would be punished on behalf of the sinner; in other words, the Savior would be put to death on a cross for sins He did not commit so that the sinner could be set free (2 Corinthians 5:21). Nearly 2,000 years ago God sent His only Son, Jesus Christ, into the world to set men free from the penalty of sin and offer eternal life to anyone who would trust in the sacrifice of His Son.

> "For God made Christ, who never sinned, to be the offering for our sin, so that we could be made right with God through Christ" (2 Corinthians 5:21, NLT).

Although Jesus was put to death for the sins of men, He did not stay in the grave. Three days following His death, Jesus was raised to life by the power of God (1 Corinthians 15:1-4) but in the same way He was resurrected from the dead, those who believe in Jesus Christ's death for sin and His resurrection, will be given eternal life (1 Corinthians 15:20-22).

According to God's divine will and plan, forgiveness of sin cannot be earned. Forgiveness is a free gift (Romans 6:23) offered to anyone who will put their faith in the death and resurrection of Jesus Christ as the payment for their sin. Maybe you feel unworthy. Maybe you feel as if your sins are too many or too extreme. The Apostle Paul makes it clear that no one is beyond forgiveness.

"If you confess with your mouth the Lord Jesus and believe in your heart that God has raised Him from the dead, you will be saved. For with the heart one believes unto righteousness, and with the mouth confession is made unto salvation. For whoever calls on the name of the Lord shall be saved." (Romans 10:9-10,13 NKJV)

Anyone who calls out to God and puts their faith in the finished work of Jesus Christ through His death and resurrection will be saved from the power and penalty (death) of sin.

Many words have been used to attempt to describe the forgiveness available to you through the sacrifice of Jesus Christ; however, listen to these simple words from the gospel of John…

"For God so loved the world that He gave His only begotten Son, that whoever believes in Him should not perish but have everlasting life. For God did not send His Son into the world to condemn the world, but that the world through Him might be saved" (John 3:16-17, NKJV).

God's love for mankind led Him to send His Son to die for the sins of men. Will you receive His love and forgiveness through trusting in Jesus' death for sin and His resurrection for the assurance of eternal life? If you've taken this first step of FAITH, please let us know by sending a message to tom@tomhogsed.co.

STEP 2: BAPTISM

After a person has believed in Jesus Christ as the One who died to pay the penalty for sin and that He resurrected to guarantee eternal life (Romans 10:9-10), it should be natural for that individual to publicly declare their faith in Jesus Christ.

Although there are many ways a person can demonstrate their faith in Jesus Christ, God ordained baptism as the way a new believer publicly shows his or her faith. New believers have been expressing their faith in Jesus Christ through baptism for nearly 2,000 years; in fact, the Apostle Peter preached a sermon to thousands of people in the first century and called on them to repent and believe in Jesus Christ (Acts 2:14-40). Those who believed were immediately baptized as an expression of their faith in Jesus (Acts 2:41).

BELIEVE and BE BAPTIZED is the pattern of identification in the early church.

The word, *baptize*, literally means to dip or immerse (in water) and the Bible teaches that a person best demonstrates their faith by being dipped or fully immersed in the water. Being fully immersed in the water is also symbolic of a person's faith in the death (person standing in the water), burial (person going under the water), and resurrection (person being raised out of the water) of Jesus Christ. So, when an individual is baptized in water, they are identifying themselves with Jesus Christ and publicly declaring their faith in Him.

According to the Bible, the only requirement before being baptized is faith in Jesus' death for sin and resurrection to secure eternal life. Once an individual makes a faith decision, they can be baptized. What if a person was baptized or sprinkled as a baby or young child? Since most babies and young children are not capable of understanding their decision to be baptized, it is important for them to wait until they have placed their faith in Jesus Christ for the forgiveness of sin and then publicly express their faith through baptism. There is nothing wrong with a parent dedicating a young child to the Lord; however, baptism is a personal decision best made when there is a clear understanding of the action. Baptism is the very first step in our obedience to Jesus Christ. Have you put your faith in Jesus Christ? Identify with Him by publicly demonstrating your faith through baptism.

ABOUT THE AUTHOR

Although Tom grew up in Charlotte, North Carolina, he currently resides in Northeast Ohio. He holds a B.A. in Youth Ministry and M.A. in Biblical Exposition. He has been married to his wife for over 20 years and they have two children. His ministry journey began when he served as a high school pastor in Ohio for nearly 14 years. In 2008, Tom and a team of 30 people planted The Summit Church (North Canton, Ohio), where he now serves as Lead Pastor. He also founded 3-A-DAY, which helps people better understand the Bible by providing resources that take approximately 3 minutes a day to read.

Tom enjoys a variety of hobbies including listening to all types of music, writing, messing with electronics, and watching British TV.

Some of the highlights of his life have been his mission travels outside of the United States to places like Mexico, Argentina, Bahamas, Peru, Dominican Republic, Italy, and Ireland. Many of these trips have made a great impact on his life.

More Info About Tom Hogsed and 3-A-DAY
Website: tomhogsed.co
Twitter: @tomhogsed
Amazon Author Page: amazon.com/author/tomhogsed
Facebook: @tomhogsed

LEAVE ME A REVIEW

If you have enjoyed using this book, consider writing a brief review. Your reviews help others who may be looking for books and resources.

Thanks for taking time to read and review!

Made in the USA
Monee, IL
15 January 2022

89002769R00080